Why not visit Hampstead Heath?

The ACE project
'Literacy for active citizenship' series

Written by Dorothy Glynn
Photographs by Ayse Hassan

Foreword

The ACE project
'Literacy for active citizenship' series

The Active Citizenship and English (ACE) project, led by Learning Unlimited and delivered in partnership with Blackfriars Settlement, Working Men's College and the Institute of Education, received funding from the European Integration Fund (July 2013 to June 2015).

The ACE project aimed to support non-EU women to develop their skills and confidence in English as well as the knowledge and confidence to take an active part in everyday life in the UK. As part of the project we wanted to produce a series of readers for our learners, and other adults also settling in the UK, which include stories about funny, personal and less typical aspects of everyday life in the UK. These books were written by learners and volunteers on the ACE project and the supporting activities have been developed by the Learning Unlimited team.

We hope you enjoy using the 'Literacy for active citizenship' series.

To find out more about the ACE project, please see:
www.learningunlimited.co/projects/ace

There are lots of lovely green spaces in London. I think Hampstead Heath is one of the most beautiful. It is in North London and it is very big. It is in the middle of London - a very busy city.

In spring the daffodils are out and there is blossom on the trees. Ducks and birds make their nests. Ducklings swim on the ponds.

There are 18 different ponds on Hampstead Heath. Some are for fishing and some are for swimming. There are separate men's and women's swimming ponds.

From Kite Hill on Hampstead Heath you can see some of the best views of London. You can see St Paul's Cathedral and the skylines of Canary Wharf and the City of London.

Hampstead Heath is very popular for sport and has an open-air swimming pool, tennis courts, an athletics track and eight different children's playgrounds. There are also cafes to meet friends and get out of the rain and cold.

There is a lot of wildlife on Hampstead Heath such as foxes, deer and swans. Parakeets fly together in colourful groups.

All year round people go to Hampstead Heath. Some brave people even swim in winter.

Why not visit Hampstead Heath?
You will love it!

Key words

athletics track	a place where people can do sports like running and jumping
blossom	flowers on trees in spring
brave	not frightened
daffodils	yellow spring flowers
deer	a wild animal with horns
ducklings	baby ducks
parakeets	small brightly coloured parrots
ponds	a small lake
skyline	the line buildings, land or sea make against the sky
wildlife	wild animal; not pets or farm animals

Questions

1. Where is Hampstead Heath?

2. What can you see and do there?

3. Where is the best place on Hampstead Heath to view London's skyline and which places what can you see from there?

4. Have you ever been to Hampstead Heath? If so, what did you see? What did you think of it?

5. Do you live near a park? What can you see there? What can you do there?

6. Do you enjoy any sports? Which ones?

7. Have you ever been swimming outside in the UK? If so, where did you swim and what was it like?

Activities

For downloadable activities, visit
www.learningunlimited.co/resources/publications

Acknowledgements

Why not visit Hampstead Heath? was written by Dorothy Glynn and photographed by Ayse Hassan. We are grateful to them for being able to include their work as part of the 'Literacy for active citizenship' series.

To find out more about Learning Unlimited, its resources and published materials, CPD and teacher training programmes, project and consultancy work, please see: **www.learningunlimited.co**